First published 1994

ISBN 0 7110 2274 7

© Peter Waller 1994

Designed by Alan C. Butcher

Published by Ian Allan Publishing

an imprint of Ian Allan Ltd, Terminal House,
Station Approach, Shepperton, Surrey TW17
8AS; and printed by Ian Allan Printing Ltd,
Coombelands House, Coombelands Lane,
Addlestone, Weybridge, Surrey KT15 1HY.

THE HEYDAY OF THE
EUROPEAN TRAM

PETER WALLER

Front Cover:

Kiel

The city of Kiel, perhaps best known as a
port city and home to the German navy, had
a sizeable 1,100mm gauge system that was
radically reduced to a single route during the
1960s despite an earlier modernisation policy
that had seen 35 new Düwag cars delivered
between 1958 and 1961. The one route,
No 4, ran for some 12km from Fähre
Holtenau to Wellingdorf. After being
threatened for many years, the route was to
be finally converted to bus operation on
4 May 1985. One of the Düwag cars, No 269,
is pictured in mid-1975. *Michael H. Waller*

Right:

Cagliari

The town of Cagliari, on the island of
Sardinia, possessed until final closure on
18 February 1973 a small electric tramway
built to the unusual gauge of 950mm. The
fleet numbered at its maximum less than 40
cars, of both four-wheel and bogie types.
Typical of the former is No 20, constructed
in 1936, which is seen in its home town in
1955. More than a decade after final closure
five of the later bogie cars were still to be
found in the depot. *H. Luff*

INTRODUCTION

Between 1945 and 1962 the electric tramcar all but disappeared from the streets of Britain. In Europe the tram has not fared so badly since the end of World War 2 although the same threats to its survival can be discerned.

In the mid-1950s there were almost 300 towns and cities in Western Europe that could lay claim to some form of tram operation. These tramways included the remaining steam trams of RTM around Rotterdam, horse tramways in Northern Ireland and on the Isle of Man, massive interurban networks like that of the SNCV in Belgium, small one or two route systems like Aarhus in Denmark, as well as the significant urban networks of cities like Hamburg, Munich, Copenhagen and Amsterdam.

Just as in Britain a decade or so earlier, the trend throughout Western Europe in the 1950s was for abandonment. It was not universal, just as in Britain in the 1930s there were numerous systems that continued to regard the tram as a cornerstone of public transport provision and invested in the tram's future. But new out-of-town housing estates required public transport and the costs involved in providing a tram service were considered prohibitive, particularly as the existing vehicles and infrastructure often required replacement at the same time. It was also an era of increased traffic congestion, congestion which the trams, running on fixed lines through the narrow city streets, were perceived as both causing and compounding. In towns and cities like Versailles and Luxembourg the 1950s and early 1960s were to witness considerable retrenchment or complete abandonment as the various pressures led the authorities to adopt alternative forms of transport — most commonly the diesel bus with its greater flexibility. As a result many systems were to disappear completely during this period. Even in cities like Amsterdam, where today the tram is regarded as the secure foundation of public transport provision, there were moves that could have led to the tram's demise. Personalities too could have an impact. The appointment of a new, bus-orientated General Manager from Danish State Railways to the municipal operator in Copenhagen led to the rapid dismembering of the city's tramway network — despite the acquisition of 100 new articulated tramcars from Düwag. Twenty years after the final conversion in the Danish capital the majority of these trams continue to give sterling service — but in Alexandria (Egypt) rather than in Denmark.

Elsewhere, the threat to the conventional tram came also from the development of metro systems as cities sought to reduce traffic congestion on the surface by sending the tram underground. Initially, many of these subways were used by conventional tramcars, but gradually the systems evolved into fully-blown metro systems. In places like Brussels and Munich, which both pursued this policy, the tramcar survives but much of the network has been replaced by newer installations.

However, just as the cost of modernising the trams in the 1950s counted against the survival of many

---

AUSTRIA

Gmunden

In the late 19th century two entrepreneurs — Stern and Hafferl — brought electric traction to a number of tramways and light railways in the Oberösterreich region of the country. The successor company's last conventional tramway is the 2.5km metre gauge tramway in Gmunden linking the spa resort with the local railway station. The line was opened on 13 August 1894 and is one of the world's steepest adhesion tramways with a maximum gradient of 1 in 10. Although the line was slightly curtailed during the 1930s and again in 1975, the link remains one of the most important of the company's operations. In July 1979 No 9 is pictured in Gmunden *en route* for the railway station. No 9 is one of two 1952-built Düwag cars acquired in 1974 from Vestische Strassenbahn in Germany. It entered service in 1977 as part of a fleet replacement programme. *Roy Brook*

systems in that period, so the cost of providing underground systems — and also public opposition in an era where environmental considerations have become stronger — has given a stay of execution to several routes and systems. There are, no doubt, going to be further casualties amongst tramway operators, but increasingly (as in Britain with the new networks in Manchester and Sheffield) there is a growing awareness that the private car and the bus are no longer capable of sustaining the requirements of urban Europe.

Forty years ago there was a remarkable variety of trams visible on the streets of Europe; as we pass through the 1990s it is pleasing to be able to comment that this variety remains. It is still possible to travel on trams of many gauges and of different generations; trams such as the Milan Peter Witt cars and the PCC cars of The Hague remain (albeit tenuously in the latter case). Elsewhere it is possible to see traditional four-wheel cars and trailers operating alongside the multi-axle articulated cars produced by Düwag and others since the late 1950s. Many of the most attractive cities in Europe retain some form of tram system and whilst the number of systems has fallen from that of the 1950s, there are still enough to justify travelling round Europe to see them.

The Heyday of the European Tram follows on from *The Heyday of the Tram*. The latter book concentrated exclusively on trams in the British Isles. This new volume, with a couple of exceptions (Blackpool — the spiritual home of the electric tram in Britain — and the Isle of Man), concentrates on the great variety of tramcar that has been visible in Europe since the late 1950s. It has not been possible to illustrate all the systems, but it is hoped that the selection made will whet the appetite and encourage more to see the European tram scene in person.

The earliest photographs selected date from the late 1950s, the most recent from 1993. Ironically one of the most recent shots illustrates one of the oldest types of car still visible, emphasising the point that it is still possible to see old style trams in Europe in everyday service outside museums.

Author's Notes
Inevitably, within the space of 80 pages it is not possible to illustrate all the tramways of Western Europe that were extant in 1960. It is hoped that readers will appreciate the selection that has been made, showing, as it does, a wide range of trams and locations from Scandinavia in the north to the Iberian Peninsula in the south. Likewise, it is not the intention to provide a detailed history of each system illustrated; this too would be impractical with a couple of hundred words. Rather, each system is given a brief historical perspective. Place names, too, cause a problem. I have attempted to use the local name, where possible, with the English equivalent if the latter is significantly different.

Acknowledgements
I am very grateful to the following people who have allowed me access to their collections for the purpose of this book: Roy Brook, David Clayre, Paul Collins, Andrew Fox, Geoff Lumb, Dick Riley and Jack Wyse. The monthly magazine *Light Rail and Modern Tramway* is an excellent means of keeping fully abreast of the latest on tramway development in Britain, Europe and the rest of the world.

Peter Waller
Ashford
January 1994

Graz
In a country dominated in scale by Wien (Vienna), Graz, in the south of the country, possesses the second largest tramway in Austria with some half dozen standard gauge lines radiating from the centre. Standard gauge horse trams were introduced to the city on 8 June 1877, and the electric tram made its first appearance on 15 June 1899. Although one route (No 2) was abandoned in 1971, the system has over the past decade seen considerable modernisation, including the acquisition of second-hand cars from Wuppertal (in the mid-1980s) to replace the fleet's older, wooden-bodied, cars. Typical of Graz's older generation of trams is No 224 seen in July 1981. One of a batch of 50 four-wheel cars built between 1949 and 1951, the majority of this type have now been replaced by the ex-Wuppertal cars. *Roy Brook*

5

Above:

Innsbruck

Apart from the independent Stubaitalbahn, there are three surviving metre gauge tram routes in Innsbruck in the Austrian Tirol. These routes are two urban lines and the lengthy rural route to Igls. However, the pioneering tramway in the town out to Solbad Hall — which opened as a steam tramway in 1891 and was electrified in 1909-10 and which became route No 4 — was abandoned in 1974 as a result of construction of a new road for the 1976 winter Olympics. The first urban route was opened in 1905 and the entire system was taken over by the municipality in 1941. Although the system survived during the early 1970s there was pressure for conversion. This was, however, resisted and a policy of modernisation and refurbishment has been followed, with several extensions proposed. Many of the cars are second-hand, such as No 31, a Düwag product of 1962 for Bielefeld in Germany, which was sold to Innsbruck in 1980. It is seen here in July 1993 at the Hungerbughbahn terminus of route No 1. *Roy Brook*

Right:

Innsbruck (Stubaitalbahn)

Although financially and legally still independent, the Stubaitalbahn is now integrated electrically (at 600V dc) into the main Innsbruck system. Dating originally from 1904, the 18.2km metre gauge line was the first high voltage single-phase ac line in Europe when it opened. From 2 July 1983 it was, however, converted to dc and operated by conventional trams from the Innsbruck fleet such as No 82 seen here in July 1984. This car is one of a batch of eight, Nos 81-8, that has a convoluted history. The end sections of each car were supplied to Hagen in the early 1960s. Sold to Innsbruck, the cars were lengthened through the incorporation of centre sections acquired from Bielefeld to create eight-axle, three-section articulated cars. *Roy Brook*

Left:

Linz

With the unusual gauge of 900mm, Linz has a tramway history stretching back more than a century. Horse cars were introduced on 1 July 1880; these were replaced by electric cars on 31 July 1897. Although a couple of routes were closed in the late 1960s and early 1970s, leading to a reduction in the route mileage to 9km by 1977, an extension of route No 1 to Auhof was opened in 1977 and further extensions have opened subsequently. From 1970 onwards more than 40 articulated cars have been acquired to replace the four-wheel cars and trailers obtained in the decade after the end of World War 2. Typical of the older generation of tram is No 1 dating from 1948 pictured on route No E — later route No 1 — in July 1973. *Roy Brook*

Right:

Linzer Lokalbahn

Another part of the Stern and Hafferl empire is the Linz Lokalbahn, a 58km route linking Linz via Eferding and Waizenkirchen to Peuerbach and Nuemarkt Kallham. The first section of this standard gauge line was opened in 1912. In 1969 as part of a fleet modernisation programme a batch of cars was obtained second-hand from Köln in Germany. Built originally in the early 1950s by Westwaggon, the cars were gradually introduced to service in Austria over a decade. One of the cars, No 22.233, is seen at Eferding in July 1981. *Roy Brook*

Far left:

Linz — Pöstlingbergbahn

Running north from the railway station at Urfahr to Pöstlingberg — a distance of just under 3km — the Pöstlingbergbahn is a metre gauge adhesion tramway. With a ruling gradient of 1 in 9, the tramway is one of the steepest adhesion lines in the world although the cars are fitted with special pincer brakes. The line first operated on 29 May 1898 and the oldest surviving open-sided cars date from that period. The majority of the fleet, such as No XII seen at Pöstlingberg in July 1981, were rebodied between 1948 and 1960. The Pöstlingbergbahn is the last tramway in Austria to use trolley poles. *Roy Brook*

Left:

Wien (Vienna)

As befits the former capital of one of the most important European empires (and still the capital city of Austria), Vienna possesses one of the largest tramway networks in the world. Although there have been closures — most notably as a result of the construction of a U-bahn network (the first section of which opened in 1976) — the city still retains a network of some 300 route km and several suburban extensions have been built. Standard gauge horse trams first appeared in the city on 4 October 1865, steam trams on 1883 and the electric tram arrived on 28 January 1897. Apart from the U-bahn, there are also a number of S-bahn routes, which were electrified from June 1925. SGP-built car No 4605 — typical of the city's modern fleet of articulated cars — which was built in 1977, is seen at the Westbahnhof terminus of route No 9 in July 1981. *Roy Brook*

Wiener Lokalbahn

Apart from the city's own network, there is also the interurban tramway of the Wiener Lokalbahn, which runs from a central terminus at Kärntner Ring — which it shares with Wien routes Nos 62 and 68 — some 30km south to Baden. Originally steam-hauled (from 29 September 1886 until 1906) electric traction was introduced on 11 May 1899. In the late 1960s a number of four-axle cars were acquired from Köln (in Germany) and from Wien. More recently, the system has obtained a number of articulated eight-axle cars, which has allowed for the withdrawal of certain of the older trams. A quartet of the ex-Köln cars is seen on Meidling Hauptstrasse in July 1981.
Roy Brook

BELGIUM

Antwerp

Horse trams first appeared on the streets of
the Belgian town of Antwerp on 26 May
1873. These were followed some 30 years
later, on 2 September 1902, with electric
trams. The tram network, considerably
expanded, continued to form the backbone of
the local transport network until the mid-
1960s when it was decided to construct a
number of subways in the central area as a
precursor to the development of a metro
system. The first section of the new subway
was opened in 1975 and development of the
network continues. To operate the existing
tramway some 166 PCC-type cars were
delivered between 1960 and 1975; one of
these, No 2052, is seen when relatively new
in April 1962. *W. J. Wyse*

Left:

Bruxelles (Brussels)

Whilst much of the investment in recent decades has gone
towards the upgrading of sections of the tramway into a metro
system, the Belgian capital retains a significant network of
routes. The first horse trams appeared on 1 May 1869
(although there had been an experimental installation more
than a decade earlier), whilst electric trams first ran in 1893.
From 1897 there were also two conduit routes, although the
last of these disappeared in 1942. The early ownership of
tramways in the city was complex, with no less than five
companies involved in the pre-electric era. Eventually the
urban routes all passed to a single operator, Tramways
Bruxellois. Although this organisation lost its concession in
1945, it was not until 1953 that the successor Société des
Transports Intercommunaux de Bruxelles (STIB) was
formally constituted. The 1950s were to see considerable
investment, with new PCC cars being constructed and the first
subways, built in connection with the Brussels Expo of 1958,
being formally opened in December 1957; the conversion of
part of the network to metro and the introduction of further
new cars gradually allowed for the withdrawal of the older
vehicles in the fleet. Typical of the pre-modernised Brussels
network are these two four-wheel cars, Nos 1410 and 3477,
which are seen in July 1965. *Roy Brook*

SNCV/NMVB

The Société Nationale des Chemins de Fer Vicinaux (or Nationale Maatschappij van Buurtspoorwegen to give its Flemish equivalent) is such a large organisation that it merits (and has*) an entire book to itself. Suffice to mention here the SNCV provided secondary public transport throughout the length and breadth of the land. It was officially created by royal decree on 1 July 1885 and in the years thereafter constructed a massive network of both steam and later electrified light railways. Inevitably much of the system has disappeared, although a number of pockets remain operational. There were a number of concentrations, one of which was around Charleroi. The SNCV's involvement in this industrial area started in 1887 with electrification arriving in 1901. Although there has been a considerable contraction, a network of routes remains and has been partially incorporated into a planned light metro scheme. Typical of the traditional SNCV is car No 9075 seen in Charleroi in July 1982. This vehicle was originally No 10283, one of a batch of metre gauge Standard cars constructed in 1938.
Roy Brook

* *100 Years of the Belgian Vicinal 1885-1985*; W. J. K. Davies, published by the LRTA.

Ghent

Although Ghent's standard gauge electric tramway network is now considerably smaller than it was in the 1930s, when it extended over some 53 route km, and the final SNCV routes were closed in 1959, there remains an impressive system in operation and one that has seen considerable investment over the past decade. The first horse trams entered service in 1874; after a brief flirtation with battery power, conventional electric tramcars appeared in 1904. By 1933 there were a total of 11 routes operational, and this remained the case until the 1950s. Over the next 20 years there were a number of conversions, although the arrival of the first of the new PCCs in 1971 was part of a reappraisal of the role of the tram. The construction of the PCCs allowed for the gradual replacement of the traditional three-axle cars, the last of which was withdrawn in 1974. One of the three-axle cars, No 326, is seen in August 1964, heading towards Moscou. *W. J. Wyse*

BRITAIN

Left:
Blackpool

One of the great ironies in British transport history is that the coastal resort of Blackpool was both the first electric tramway in Britain — opening on 29 September 1885 — and also the last conventional tramway on the mainland. Although the first town routes were abandoned during the 1930s and the last — the North station route — in 1963, the long sea front route from Starr Gate to Fleetwood remains operational. That Blackpool did not disappear completely is, perhaps, the result of the foresight of one man — Walter Luff — the system's General Manager from 1933 until 1954. In his first two years the fleet was largely modernised through the acquisition of streamlined cars produced by English Electric and Brush and it is these cars, in many cases substantially rebuilt, that still form the core of the modern Blackpool fleet. Typical of those cars acquired during the 1930s is No 625 seen at the southern (Starr Gate) terminus in 1975. This was one of a batch of 20 built by Brush — the last trams built by the company — in 1937. This car is still in service almost 60 years after construction — a remarkable tribute to the planning of one man. *Michael H. Waller*

Right:
Snaefell Mountain Railway

Of the five 'traditional' tramways to survive in Britain, three are on the Isle of Man. Apart from the 3ft 0in Douglas horse trams and the similarly gauged cars of the Manx Electric, there is also the 3ft 6in gauge Snaefell Mountain Railway linking the MER at Laxey with the peak of the 2,100ft mountain. Opened on 21 August 1895, the Snaefell Mountain Railway utilises a central third track for braking purposes following the designs patented by G. Noble Fell. Six cars were supplied by Milnes at the opening, five of which survive in service. The sixth was burnt out in 1971 and rebuilt. On 22 July 1964 car No 1 is seen at Laxey. In the background is Manx Electric Railway No 27, a crossbench power car built by Milnes in 1898. *Geoff Lumb*

16

DENMARK

Aarhus

That the small two route system in Denmark's second city of Aarhus remained until final closure on 19 November 1971 was nothing short of miraculous, considering that the entire fleet of 47 power cars and trailers had been destroyed by fire in the depot as a result of bombing by Danish partisans on 22 August 1944. The fleet was, however, to be rebuilt and a total of 20 four-wheel cars and 19 trailers survived to operate over the 14km of metre gauge route. Services were restored in July 1945 using 12 rebuilt power cars and 13 rebuilt trailers. A further eight power cars and six trailers were acquired in 1948. Horse trams ran in the city between 1883 and 1895 and the electric network was inaugurated over a short route on 4 July 1904. Following the municipal take-over in 1928 the route was extended and a second line opened. Three months prior to closure, on 12 August 1971, power car No 18 (later to become the last car in passenger service) and trailer No 59 (both of which were amongst the vehicles delivered in 1948) are seen at the Kongsvang terminus of route No 2.
Michael H. Waller

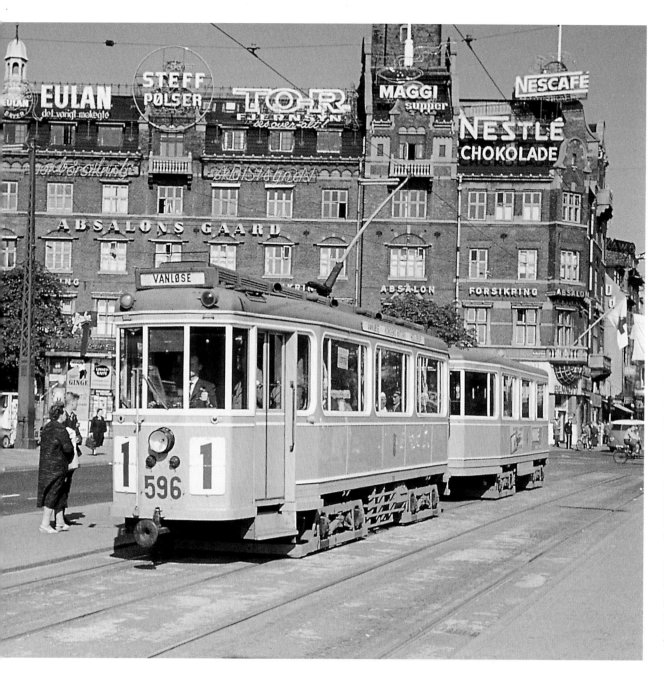

København (Copenhagen)

Trams were to appear very early in the Danish capital, with the first horse trams operating on 22 October 1863. From this single route a considerable network, controlled by a number of companies, sprang up. Steam trams appeared in the city during the 1880s and electric traction first ran using (curiously) accumulator cars in 1897. Conventional electric trams appeared in 1899 and the conversion of the system proceeded rapidly. The system continued to develop and, in 1911, the trams within the city area were taken over by the municipality. Further expansion and fleet modernisation followed in the 1920s. Although there were plans for further extensions in the 1950s only one was completed and there were also a number of abandonments later in the decade, but the acquisition of a batch of Düwag articulated cars from 1960 onwards seemed to augur well for the future. However, a change of policy led to the rapid conversion of the system, with the final closure taking place in April 1972. Ironically, the Düwag cars continue to give service in Egypt. In September 1960, bogie power car No 596, one of a batch built between 1930 and 1941 and rebuilt in the 1950s, is seen on route No 1 to Vanløse. *W. J. Wyse*

FINLAND

Helsingfors (Helsinki)

The Finnish capital city has an extensive tramway network and, despite the construction of a metro, has plans for the future development of the tramway network well into the next century. Horse trams first operated in the city on 11 December 1890.

Electric tram services were introduced on 4 September 1900 and the last horse tram ran on 21 October 1901. There are a total of 11 routes currently operated and the fleet comprises more than 100 cars, of which the majority are articulated. The first of the articulated cars were delivered in 1973 and the introduction of the new cars allowed for the withdrawal of the last four-wheel cars by

1975 and the cessation of trailer operation in 1983. The only non-articulated cars remaining in service are a number of the bogie cars, Nos 1-30, which were delivered in 1959. One of these cars is pictured on a tour in the autumn of 1967. *Frank Hunt Collection/Courtesy LRTA London Area*

Turku (Åbo)

Horse trams, to the unusual gauge of 1,436mm, first appeared on the streets of Turku on 4 May 1890. But this service was destined to be shortlived and was withdrawn on 31 October 1892. Sixteen years later, on 22 December 1908 metre gauge electric trams were inaugurated. The system continued to develop through until the 1930s. Despite serious damage during the war, the tramway survived and, following further alterations, a basic pattern of three routes was established. A final extension was opened in 1956. However, despite the modernisation of the 1950s the system was to contract rapidly between 1967 and the final closure in October 1972. Here bogie power car No 50, one of a batch of eight delivered in 1956, is seen with 1946-built trailer car No 125 in the summer of 1967. *Frank Hunt Collection/Courtesy LRTA London Area*

FRANCE

Electrique Lille Roubaix Tourcoing (ELRT)

There was a complex network of lines serving the Lille region. Part of this was an urban network serving Lille itself, which was finally converted to bus operation in 1966, whilst serving the area beyond the city is the metre gauge ELRT. The first section of what was to form the ELRT opened as a standard gauge horse tramway on 19 March 1877. The line was electrified and the gauge converted during the 1890s and, by 1929, after the take-over of the urban lines in Roubaix and Tourcoing, the company reached its peak of 231 trams operating over 120 km of route. All the urban routes were converted between 1951 and 1956 leaving the main Lille-Roubaix/Tourcoing routes with the short branch to Marcq (abandoned on 5 September 1972). Seen in Roubaix in July 1974 is No 515, one of a batch of 28 built by Brissoneau et Lotz in 1950. It is seen in the red and ivory livery introduced in 1971. These cars have now been replaced by second-hand cars acquired from Germany. In Lille itself the successor to ELRT — which combined with the municipal operator in 1982 — now runs in a short tunnel to connect with the new rubber-tyred VAL (Véhicule Automatique Léger) metro. *Roy Brook*

22

Lille

The urban trams in Lille, which overlapped the area operated by ELRT, were initially operated by the Tramways Electriques de Lille et de sa Banlieue (TELB). The first section of what was later to form TELB opened as a horse tramway in February 1874 under the aegis of Tramways du Nord. After a period with steam operation, electric trams were introduced in 1902. The standard gauge system grew to a maximum of 21 routes operating over 103km of track. TELB's franchise expired in 1956 and it was replaced by a new operator Compagnie Générale Industrielle de Transports (CGIT). The policy of the new operator was the replacement of the trams by buses and the first conversion under CGIT took place on 15 July 1956. There remained 100 trams in service at the end of 1957 but conversion proceeded rapidly during the early 1960s and the last route was replaced by buses on 31 January 1966. Two of the fleet's four-wheel cars, Nos 810 and 832 (dating from the 1930s), are seen in April 1962. *W. J. Wyse*

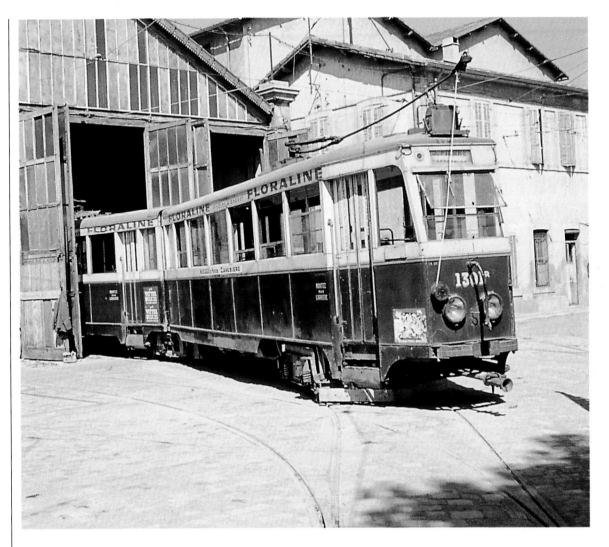

Marseille

The single surviving tramway route at Marseille is a remarkable remnant of a standard gauge network that once extended over some 170 route km. Horse trams first arrived in 1873 and electric cars in 1890. In 1949 a total of 32 routes were in operation but by 1960 this had been reduced to route No 68 alone. This 3.2km route had an interesting history as it was originally a steam railway and was converted to electric traction in 1905. Its survival after the withdrawal of the remaining system was a result of an 800m subway forming its city terminus. In 1968-69 the existing fleet was replaced by 16 new PCC cars. The earlier Marseille fleet is shown by No 1301, an experimental articulated car of 1949, which is seen in August 1958. *Photographer Unknown/W. J. Wyse Collection*

St Etienne

The city of St Etienne is a further French example of where tramway operation has been reduced to a single route. As with both Marseille and Lille, there are particular local reasons for the survival of this one route beyond the early 1950s when the other tram routes in the city were converted primarily to trolleybus operation. These factors included the frequency of service and the fact that the route operated in both directions down a street that was effectively one-way only. The surviving route, some four miles in length, connects Bellevue with Terrasses. Dating originally to the early 1880s as a metre gauge steam tramway, it was to form part of the CFVE (Compagnie des Chemins de Fer à Voie Etroite de Saint-Etienne, Firminy, Rive-de-Gier et Extensions). A second tramway operation, Tramways Electriques de Saint-Etienne (TE), was established in 1896. The CFVE was electrified from 1907 onwards. Both operators commenced a programme of tramcar replacement; the last TE trams operated in 1951. Following the decision to retain the single route, 30 PCC-type trams were acquired in 1958-59 and a further five in 1967. More recently, a batch of articulated cars have been delivered and the route also slightly extended. Typical of the CFVE's green fleet is trailer car No S19 seen in August 1958. *W. J. Wyse Collection*

Valenciennes

Close to Lille there was a sprawling network of some 40 route km of metre gauge trams operated by the Chemins de Fer Economiques du Nord. This system had its origins as a series of steam railways constructed from the 1880s onwards. Electrification took place immediately prior to the start of World War 1 and, apart from the construction of a new tramway station at Valenciennes in the mid-1950s, little changed thereafter. The system remained largely intact until the late 1950s with six routes being operated with a fleet of some 40 power cars and some 80 trailers. Conversion started in earnest in 1963 and the last route, to Bonsecours, was closed on 1 July 1966. Typical of the Valenciennes operation is this view of four-wheel power car No 5 and two trailers pictured on a tour in April 1962. *W. J. Wyse*

GERMANY

Aachen

The border city of Aachen possessed both a large tramway and trolleybus network. However, the significant metre gauge urban and interurban system had been reduced to one single route by the early 1970s. This route linked the Dutch frontier at Vaals, via the city centre, with Brand. Seen in the operator's red and cream livery is No 1014, one of six cars acquired from Mönchen-Gladbach in 1967. This car, formerly Mönchen-Gladbach No 28, was eventually sold to Mainz, where a couple of sister cars remain in service. It is seen here in Aachen in July 1970. The Aachen trams were finally to be converted to bus operation on 29 September 1974. *Roy Brook*

Above:

Augsburg

The three route, metre gauge system in Augsburg was modernised during the mid- and late- 1960s through the acquisition or rebuilding of a fleet of unusual five-axle articulated cars. In 1992-93 the fleet was supplemented through the acquisition of a number of ex-Stuttgart four-axle cars built by Maschinenfabrik Esslingen and dating from 1959-61. One of these second-hand purchases, No 403, is seen in its new home town in July 1993. *Roy Brook*

Right:

Bonn

The capital of the old Federal Republic of West Germany, Bonn retains both a standard gauge urban and interurban tramway network, although many of the street sections in the town centre have been replaced by subways. In 1957 a fleet modernisation programme was started through the acquisition of new Düwag four-axle cars. Over the next decade almost 50 bogie and articulated trams were acquired, the majority of which remain in service at the time of writing. Older cars have, however, been replaced by newer Düwag models for use over the Stadtbahn lines. One of the first of the Düwag cars is seen, when new, in July 1957. *Roy Brook*

Bremen

With its first section opening on 22 June 1890, the standard gauge system of Bremen is one of the oldest electric tramways in Germany and one of the longest lasting.

Significant investment over the past 30 years has seen the entire fleet replaced and numerous extensions opened. Typical of the existing Bremen fleet is Hansa-built four-axle car No 414 dating from 1962 seen in July 1972 at the terminus of route No 2 at Gröpelingen. Many of these cars will be replaced during the mid-1990s by 108 new trams ordered in 1992. *Roy Brook*

Bremerhaven

Bremerhaven was one of a number of German tramway operators which witnessed severe contraction during the 1960s leaving only one standard gauge route operational by the early 1970s. However, this one route — from Langen to the main railway station — was to survive until final closure on 30 July 1982. Exactly a decade before closure, in July 1972, two articulated units, headed by Hansa-built four-axle car No 81 of 1968, are seen in the operator's attractive cream and red livery. *Roy Brook*

Braunschweig

With its first section of electric tramway opening on 28 October 1897, the 1,100mm gauge system at Braunschweig remains operational with, in 1992, some 50 power cars and some 25 trailers constructed by Düwag and Linke-Hofmann-Busch. This was another system that underwent slight contraction in the late 1960s, but reversed the policy in the early 1970s and witnessed a number of extensions. Düwag-built car No 35 of 1962, a six-axle articulated car, is seen in July 1972 on the intermediate loop at Rühme on route No 2. This car, now renumbered 6267, remains in service.
Roy Brook

Darmstadt

The small metre gauge tramway network at Darmstadt commenced operation on 24 November 1897 and, almost a century later, a modernised system survives. Apart from three relatively short lines radiating from Luisenplatz, the bulk of the system is represented by three longer routes north, east and south of the town. Of these, the longest, at some 15km in length, is that to Alsbach. Between 1954 and 1956 nine four-wheel cars, Nos 11-19, were supplied to the operator by Rathgeber. One of these, No 15 (which remained in service in 1992), is seen in July 1969 on route No 6 heading through the town *en route* for the Hauptbahnhof. *Roy Brook*

Above:

Dortmund

Situated on the fringes of the Ruhr, the standard gauge tramway system of Dortmund has seen dramatic alterations over the past decade. Although many of the suburban routes have long single-track sections, the construction of subways in the central area (which first opened in the 1980s) and the development of the Ruhr Stadtbahn scheme has ensure the survival of the system with some 98 articulated cars delivered from Düwag since 1981. 1994 sees the centenary of electric tramcar operation in the town; the first cars operated on 1 March 1894. Two of an earlier generation of Düwag-built articulated cars, No 33 (now withdrawn) and 37 of 1966 are seen at the terminus of the long route No 1 to Brambauer. Although this route was threatened with closure, it now forms part of the upgraded system as route No U45. *Roy Brook*

Right:

Esslingen (END)

The small metre gauge system of one main route and branch, which served Esslingen, Nellingen and Denkendorf, was controlled by the operator of the trams in Stuttgart. Although the main route closed in the mid-1970s, the branch from Nellingen (where the single depot was situated) to Neuhausen was to survive until replacement by buses on 20 February 1978. Five years earlier, in July 1973, No 5, one of a batch of four-axle cars supplied by Maschinenfabrik Esslingen in the late 1920s for the line's opening, is seen at the northern terminus of Esslingen station. *Roy Brook*

Flensburg

Below:

The northernmost town in Germany to possess an electric tramway was Flensburg, just south of the Danish border. Originally served by a standard gauge horse tramway, which opened in May 1881 and was converted to metre gauge in 1889, metre gauge electric trams made their appearance on 6 July 1907. The conversion to bus operation was completed on 2 June 1973. Here four-wheel car No 38, built by Crede in 1952, is seen with a MaK trailer operating over the system's solitary remaining route in July 1972. *Roy Brook*

Frankfurt am Main

Right:

Frankfurt am Main, like many large German cities has, over the past few decades witnessed a considerable revolution as the traditional street tramway has been replaced with upgraded Stadtbahn and U-bahn lines. The first section of combined tram/Stadtbahn subway opened in 1968 and further sections have followed, reducing the standard gauge tram network to a fraction of its former size. In July 1970 the traditional street cars reigned supreme, however. Seen outside the Hauptbahnhof are Düwag-built No 483 of 1953 (with a four-wheel trailer) on route No 21 to the Westbahnhof and 1963-built (also by Düwag) No 635 on route No 25 to Heddenheim. Although both cars have now been withdrawn, the remainder of the 1963-built cars remained in service in 1992. *Roy Brook*

Gleis 1 bis 8
Stühlinger

Freiburg im Bresgau

Although relatively small, the metre gauge tramway in the southwest German town has seen a number of extensions and considerable fleet replacement over the past two decades. Electric trams were introduced to the town's streets on 14 October 1901 and, by 1992, a total of five routes were in operation with a fleet of some 50 cars, the majority of which are Düwag eight-axle articulated cars. Two of the type are seen passing at the Hauptbahnhof, where an improved interchange has been constructed. The steep gradients associated with the ramps for the new interchange required that all eight axles of the articulated cars be powered. *Roy Brook*

Hagen

Electric tram cars first appeared on the streets of Hagen on 18 November 1896. Although a fleet of new cars was acquired between 1954 and 1967, a closure policy was instituted which led to the rapid contraction of the system until final closure on 29 May 1976. One of the Düwag-built six-axle articulated cars, dating from the early 1960s, is seen in July 1971 running over route No 7 to Markt outside the Hauptbahnhof. On the adjacent track is Düwag-built four-wheel car No 127 dating from the mid-1950s.
Roy Brook

37

Above:

Hamburg

The once massive standard gauge system of the port city of Hamburg was gradually closed in favour of both U-bahn and Stadtbahn systems. By the early 1970s the system had contracted to barely half a dozen routes and the last of these were converted on 1 October 1978. In July 1972 bogie car No 3334, dating from 1954, is seen heading towards the Hauptbahnhof on route No 1.
Roy Brook

Right:

Hannover

The city of Hannover retains an impressive standard gauge tramway, with a number of central area subways, the first of which opened in the mid-1970s. In the early 1970s it was the intention that these subways would form part of a U-bahn network, but 20 years on conventional trams remain. Over recent years the system has been significantly extended and many new eight-axle articulated cars introduced. Hannover was also the centre for a network of interurban routes, although only one of these now remains operational — route No 1 to Sarstedt. The first electric trams operated in the city on 19 May 1893. Between 1895 and 1903 the city also witnessed the operation of battery-powered trams. Seen outside the opera house in July 1977 is Düwag-built four-axle car No 471, which is one of a batch of cars delivered between 1956 and 1958. These cars have now been withdrawn, although sister car No 478 remains as part of the museum fleet. *Roy Brook*

Heidelberg

A metre gauge electric tramway opened in Heidelberg on 17 March 1902 replacing an older, standard gauge, horse tramway. A programme of closures begun in the 1960s saw the system reduced to four routes by the 1990s, with a jointly owned line linking the town with Mannheim. Pictured in the blue and white livery of the undertaking in July 1969, No 211 was built by Düwag in 1961. Withdrawn two years after the date of the photograph, the car was sold to Mainz where it remains in service. *Roy Brook*

Karlsruhe

The town of Karlsruhe possessed both a standard gauge urban network and a metre gauge interurban route. The latter — the Albtalbahn — was modernised between 1958 and 1961 to standard gauge and, like the urban network, has been significantly extended over the past 20 years. In July 1970 six-axle articulated car No 158, one of a batch delivered between 1959 and 1964, heads south from Marktplatz on route No 2. The Neureuter Strasse route has subsequently been extended to Siemensalle, although it is not now served by trams on No 2. By 1992 No 158 was in store, although other members of the type remain in service. *Roy Brook*

Left:
Kassel
The standard gauge system serving Kassel has undergone, over the past 30 years, considerable investment with the building of a tram subway outside the Hauptbahnhof (opened in 1968) and several extensions and the acquisition of new vehicles. A total of some 160 power cars and trailers have been obtained from various manufacturers (most recently Düwag) since 1966. Seen at Am Stern where the system possesses a 'Grand Union' junction, in July 1972 is Wegmann/Düwag-built car No 317. This is one of three six-axle cars acquired in 1970.
Roy Brook

Right:
Köln (Cologne)
Köln, with a number of significant sections of tram subway opening from 1968 onwards, retains a large and important standard gauge tramway with a fleet of over 300 trams. Horse trams first appeared in the city on 28 April 1877, surviving until 22 May 1907, whilst the first electric trams operated on 15 October 1901. Köln is also the home of the Köln-Bonner Eisenbahn, which provides a link between Köln and Bonn. The KBE's two routes have recently been integrated into the Köln municipal operation. Seen in Neumarkt in July 1958 is the recently newly delivered four-wheel power car No 1015 on route No G to Berg Gladbach. The last cars of this type were withdrawn in the early 1970s.
Roy Brook

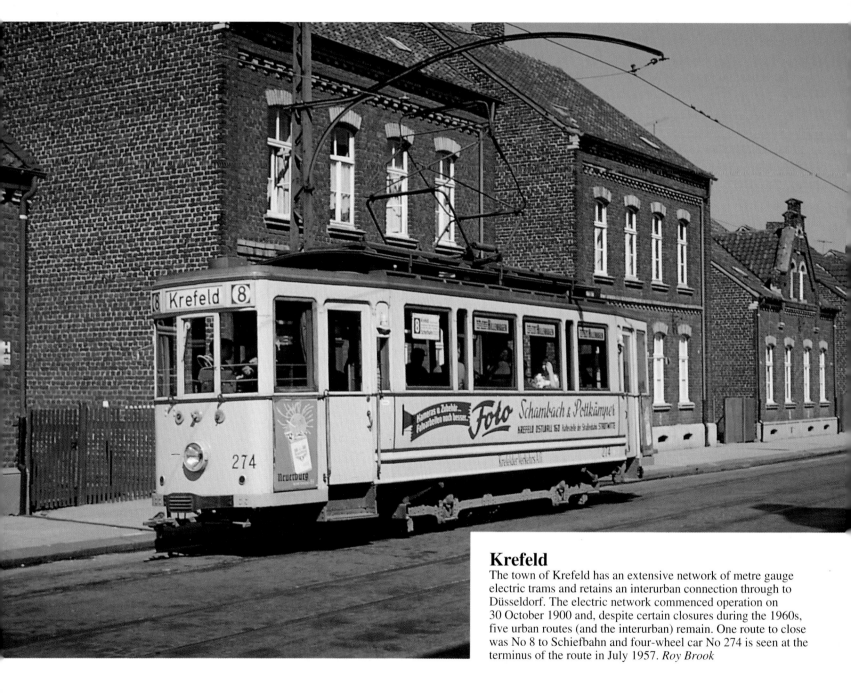

Krefeld

The town of Krefeld has an extensive network of metre gauge electric trams and retains an interurban connection through to Düsseldorf. The electric network commenced operation on 30 October 1900 and, despite certain closures during the 1960s, five urban routes (and the interurban) remain. One route to close was No 8 to Schiefbahn and four-wheel car No 274 is seen at the terminus of the route in July 1957. *Roy Brook*

Mainz

Although the metre gauge network that served Mainz was reduced to a much smaller system of effectively four lines radiating from the centre by the early 1970s, investment since then has seen a number of extensions into outlying suburbs. In July 1974 No 211 is seen at the Hauptbahnhof running on route No 8 to Bretzenheim. During the 1970s and 1980s the Mainz fleet was strengthened through the acquisition of trams from other operators, most notably Heidelberg and Aachen. No 211 was one of six Düwag cars acquired from the latter in 1973; prior to service in Aachen, they had originally operated in Mönchen-Gladbach. *Roy Brook*

Left:

Mülheim-an-der-Ruhr

Dating originally from 8 July 1897, the history of the metre gauge tram network in Mülheim-an-der-Ruhr is closely interlinked with that of the neighbouring systems such as Essen. In the later 1960s closure of certain routes was the result of the abandonment of the neighbouring Oberhausen system, whilst the opening of the first subway in 1972 was to facilitate the later construction of the standard gauge Ruhr Stadtbahn network. Apart from the Stadtbahn link to Essen, there are also a number of through tram services linking the towns, and there is also a standard gauge line to Duisburg. In July 1987, No 229 a Düwag-built car of 1955 is seen on route No 114 to Grenze Borbreck. This represents a short working on one of the through routes to Essen. *Roy Brook*

Right:

München (Munich)

Over the past 20 years the standard gauge trams in the Bavarian capital of München have been progressively replaced by a new network of U-bahn lines. The first of these opened in 1971 and since then six lines have been completed with further additions planned. Despite this, however, the city retains a sizeable traditional tramway network. In July 1969, before the commencement of the U-bahn programme, three-axle car No 1024 is seen on route No 8 to Fürstenried-Ost. This car was one of a batch of 40 built by Rathgeber in 1964 (Nos 1010-49) which were renumbered to Nos 2601-20/51-70 in 1971-72. The whole batch remains in service. The route to Fürstenried-Ost has, however, been converted to U-bahn operation and now forms part of route No U3. *Roy Brook*

Ober Rheinische Eisenbahn Gesellschaft

With its first section opening on 2 September 1915, the metre gauge OEG continues to operate a small network of interurban lines around Heidelberg and Mannheim. The tramway is owned by these two towns and by the adjacent town of Weinheim. In July 1974 eight-axle articulated car No 104, built by Uerdingen the previous year to a design by Düwag, is seen at the OEG's Mannheim terminus awaiting departure on the circular route A which runs via Weinheim and Heidelberg before returning to Mannheim. *Roy Brook*

Neunkirchen

Until its closure on 11 June 1978
Neunkirchen im Saarland could lay claim to
possessing the smallest electric tramway in
the old West Germany. Dating originally
from September 1907, eight four-axle cars
were supplied to the system as fleet
replacements in 1962 by Maschinenfabrik
Esslingen, although one (No 7) was later
scrapped after an accident. The first of these
cars, No 1, is seen in the town in July 1977.
Effectively only one route (from Schlacthof
to Steinwald) with a short branch, the
system's total length was only some five
kilometres. The route's survival was due to a
steep hill in the town, which was considered
to be unsafe for buses in wintry weather.
Roy Brook

Above:

Recklinghausen-Bottrop

Although the fleet of Vestische Strassenbahn Gmbh, which operated a network of metre gauge routes to the north of Essen and Bochum serving the towns of, inter alia, Recklinghausen, Herten, Horst and Bottrop, underwent significant modernisation during the late 1950s and early 1960s, a reversal of policy led to a number of the routes being closed and the remainder being converted as part of the Ruhr Stadtbahn scheme. Final closure of the conventional tramway network, which had first operated on 26 February 1892, was on 30 October 1982. Much of the fleet was sold for further service on the ELRT in France. Car No 357, a four-axle car built by Düwag in 1954, is seen in Recklinghausen in July 1971. *Roy Brook*

Right:

Reutlingen

Although the metre gauge Reutlingen system, which dated originally from 1912, had undergone considerable modernisation in the late 1950s and early 1960s, a policy of abandonment led to the conversion of the northern half of the system in 1970. Although the southern two routes were scheduled for conversion in 1971, in the event road construction delayed the final closure until 19 October 1974. One of the system's 1963-built XM4d articulated cars is seen at the southern terminus of route No 2, Pfüllingen, in July 1973. *Roy Brook*

Right:

Rhein-Haardtbahn

The Rhein-Haardtbahn is a metre gauge interurban line jointly owned by the Ludwigshafen and Mannheim undertakings. Its main line links Mannheim with Bad Dürkheim and there is also a shorter branch from Ludwigshafen to Oppau. The fleet, all supplied by Düwag, was completely replaced between 1959 and 1967 and, in 1992, comprised some 13 power cars and eight trailers. No 1021, seen at Bad Dürkheim in July 1970 was one of two 12-axle articulated cars delivered in 1967.
Roy Brook

Left:

Siegburg

Kleinbahn Siegburg Zündorf was a standard gauge interurban. It was one of a number controlled from Essen by the Rheinisch-Westfailisch Strassen und Kleinbahn Gesellschaft which closed during the 1960s. This particular line opened on 19 March 1914 and closed in stages during the early 1960s. The section between Siegburg and Sieglar was replaced by buses on 14 October 1963, whilst the final part, that between Sieglar and Wahn closed on 31 August 1965. Latterly, although operated each day, services were infrequent. The fleet by the early 1960s numbered nine power cars and seven trailers. In July 1957 power car No 2 is seen at the Zündorf terminus. In the distance is the terminus of the route to Köln operated by Kölner Verkehrs-Betriebe. *Roy Brook*

Stuttgart

The metre gauge electric tramway in Stuttgart, which was amongst the first in Germany (opening in 1895), has over the past 30 years seen considerable changes. The first of the central area subways were opened in 1966 and many sections have subsequently been upgraded to form a standard gauge U-bahn network. There were also significant extensions to the narrow gauge network to outlying suburbs, although the process of upgrading continues. In July 1969, whilst the traditional tram reigned supreme, Maschinenfabrik Esslingen-built No 524 of 1959 is see outside the Hauptbahnhof on route No 6 towards Echterdingen. *Roy Brook*

Above:

Stuttgart

Apart from the conventional metre gauge system, Stuttgart also possesses a short rack tramway from Degerloch to Marienplatz. Until replacement in 1982, the line was operated by a small batch of four-wheel cars with trailers. The oldest of the power cars, which were all built by Maschinenfabrik Esslingen, dated from 1935, although two were built in 1950. In August 1969 No 102 (which was shortly to be withdrawn) is seen at Degerloch. At that time the route was numbered 30; it is now route No 10 and is served by a trio of MAN-built four-axle cars. *Roy Brook*

Right:

Ulm

Although reduced by the early 1970s to a single route — No 1 from Söflingen to Friedrichsau — the trams continue to operate in Ulm. In July 1973, the date of this shot, the system possessed 10 four-axle power cars, Nos 1-10, supplied by Maschinenfabrik Esslingen in 1958 and 15 trailers, Nos 51-65, supplied by Fuchs in 1953. Here No 8 is seen at the intermediate loop at Stadion in the operator's yellow, black and white livery. The power cars, which had an unusual arrangement of control equipment and body-suspended motors, were replaced by second-hand cars acquired from Stuttgart in the mid-1980s. *Roy Brook*

Left:

Wuppertal

Although better known as the home of the Schwebebahn, or suspended monorail, Wuppertal could also lay claim to a dual gauge tramway network. Chronologically the first electric trams to operate in the town were those of the metre gauge system, which opened on 16 April 1894. The standard gauge was not long in following, being opened on 1 September the same year. Both continued until the metre gauge routes were converted to bus operation on 31 July 1970. The 1960s also witnessed a contraction in the standard gauge network, but the final section was not to be converted to bus operation until 30 May 1987 — the most recent casualty to the motorbus in the country. Four-wheel car No 231, dating from the 1920s, is seen in July 1957 awaiting departure from the Tolleturm terminus with a service on the standard gauge route No 14 to Opernhaus. This particular route was one of the casualties of the 1960 closures. *Roy Brook*

Right:

Wurzburg

The small metre gauge system at Wurzburg has, over the past few years, seen a considerable expansion with the significant extension of route No 5 southwards to Athener Ring/Stauffenbergstrasse with a further extension planned to Rottenbauer. In addition new articulated cars have replaced older vehicles. Horse trams first appeared in Wurzburg on 8 April 1892. Electric cars followed on 30 June 1900, but these ceased operation on 20 April 1920. Electric trams reappeared on 18 September 1924. No 270, a Düwag-built six-axle articulated car of 1962 awaits departure from the Zellerau terminus of routes Nos 2 and 4 in July 1980. *Roy Brook*

ITALY

Genova (Genoa)

The port city of Genova, with steep hills and narrow coastal shoreline, was a nightmare for the transport planner and, thus, saw the development of both tramways and funiculars. Horse trams first appeared in the 1870s and metre gauge electric trams in the mid-1890s. Initially three companies owned the emerging electric tramways, but these were eventually united into a single company and, from 1928, the shares in this company slowly passed into municipal ownership. Post 1928 there was considerable modernisation, but, in January 1956, the decision was made to convert the system to bus and trolleybus. Although some 20 routes and 250 trams were operational in 1964, the last tram ran on 26 December 1966. One of the features of the system was the Galleria della Certosa, a 1,761m long tunnel, which, when opened in 1908, was the longest tram tunnel in the world. When closed in October 1964, this was converted into a bus tunnel, but it was later to form the basis of a new Light Rail scheme that commenced operation in June 1990. In May 1963 car No 831 (one of a batch rebuilt from trailer cars in 1934) is seen emerging from the tunnel's north portal.
Photographer Unknown/W. J. Wyse Collection

Milan

The northern city of Milan has one of Italy's largest tramway networks. With electric trams first appearing in 1893, the system underwent considerable modernisation in the late 1920s as a result of the change of rule of road from left-hand to right-hand running in 1926. Contemporary with this change through routes were established and the opportunity was taken to replace the fleet with cars based on the latest US practice — the Peter Witt cars as used in cities like Cleveland and Philadelphia. These cars were designed to maximise passenger flow through the use of a seated conductor. The prototype cars, Nos 1501 and 1502, were built by Società Italiana Carminati & Toselli of Milan and a further 500 cars were ordered in 1928. In 1931 the trams, previously owned by a subsidiary of the Edison company, were taken over by the municipality and, despite the appearance of the first of some 200 articulated cars in 1955, there remain some 350 Peter Witt cars in service. No 1757, typical of the type, is seen on route No 19 to P. Negrelli in early 1993. *Andrew J. Fox*

Left:
Naples

The once extensive tramway system in the south Italian city of Naples, which originated as a horse tramway in 1875 with electric cars first appearing in 1899, underwent considerable contraction in the 1960s. By 1967 only five routes remained operational with a fleet of some 100 bogie cars in service. Although a number of these trams were rebuilt in the late 1970s, further contraction led to the system being reduced to but a single route by late 1981. However, two routes were reintroduced in 1983 and the tram continues to survive. Typical of the Naples fleet is No 981 (now withdrawn) which is seen in Riviera Di Chiaia on 11 June 1961. These cars dated originally from the mid-1930s and were later rebuilt.
W. J. Wyse Collection

Right:
Rome (ATAC)

The recent history of municipally-owned trams in Rome has been variable. Although reaching a peak of 57 routes, with 131km of route mileage and a fleet of 570 motor cars and 250 trailers in 1929, some 40km of that was abandoned on 1 January 1930 due to the creation of a new route organisation based on a number of circular routes. Earlier Rome had seen its first standard gauge horse tram on 2 August 1877. The first, privately owned, electric trams operated on 19 September 1895 and the first municipal trams ran on 22 March 1911. By 1929 all the routes were municipally operated. Despite further closures occasioned by the revised traffic arrangements for the 1960 Olympics some 15 routes remained in operation in 1964, although further routes were to close during the 1960s. The 1970s witnessed contradictory policies with abandonments and reinstatements on a regular basis as investment went into the construction of an underground system. However, the tram survives — just — in Rome. Constructed by Fiat in the early 1930s, No 2199, seen here on 8 April 1978, was typical of much of the Rome fleet of the late 1970s.

Peter Waller

LUXEMBOURG

Luxembourg

The small state of Luxembourg could lay claim to possessing one of the most attractive small tramways in Europe. Its origins lay in a standard gauge horse tramway that commenced operation on 20 February 1875. The system was taken over by the municipality in 1906 and converted to a metre gauge electric tramway. This was inaugurated on 8 August 1908. It continued to expand until 1930, when it reached a peak of 30.9 route km. Although the twisting streets of the town lent themselves to tramway operation, declining finances led to the first withdrawals in November 1951. In 1952 the fleet comprised 34 power cars and 19 trailers. From the mid-1950s conversion became more rapid and the final route was converted to bus operation on 5 September 1964. Original trailer car No 101, seen in the attractive cobalt blue livery in April 1962, was originally a horse tram and was converted to act as a trailer in 1908.

W. J. Wyse

Left:
Amsterdam
The largest of the three surviving traditional tramways in the Netherlands is that in Amsterdam. Electric trams first appeared in the city on 14 August 1900 and by World War 2 a large network had been established. However, postwar uncertainty led to a partial conversion to bus operation during the 1950s and it was only in 1957, with the unveiling of the first articulated tram and the decision to extend the system to serve the new suburb of Osdorp in the early 1960s, that the tram was given a secure future in the city. Since the early 1960s Amsterdam has witnessed a considerable investment in both infrastructure and vehicles and now boasts a fleet of some 250 articulated trams. Typical of this modern fleet is No 645, a product of Beijnes in 1963, en route to Centraal station in the old style grey and white livery. *R.C. Riley*

Below:
Den Haag (The Hague)
The Hague is the administrative centre of the Netherlands; it can also lay claim to the first tramway in the country — a horse tram route linking it with the coast at Scheveningen opened on 23 June 1864. Electric trams first appeared on the city's streets in 1904 and a significant network of urban routes grew up. The Hague was also the centre of a network of interurban routes although all these, bar the line to Delft, were converted by the early 1960s. The last interurban route was converted to 600V dc in 1965 and integrated into the city's network; it survives to this day. Although, as elsewhere, the tide seemed to have turned against the tram in the city, a reversal of policy led to the expansion of the network with route extensions and the building of reserved track alignments. The Hague could, at one time, lay claim to one of the largest fleets of PCCs (Presidents' Conference Car — derived from US practice) in Europe, but the last of these were withdrawn from everyday service in 1993 being replaced by a new fleet of articulated cars (which, to save cost, incorporated certain parts from the withdrawn PCCs). Typical of The Hague PCCs is No 1333 seen on the coast on route No 11 on 25 October 1989. This car was one of a batch of 40 (Nos 1301-40) delivered to The Hague from La Brugeoise between 1971 and 1974. *Peter Waller*

NZH

The blue trams of the Noord-Zuid
Hollandsche Vervoer Maatschappij
represented, until their final demise in 1961,
one of the greatest of European interurban
tramway networks. The system comprised
both metre and standard gauge lines and was
the result of the merger of some 11 different
companies. Many of these lines had their
origins in steam tramways, which only
became legal in the Netherlands in 1879,
whilst others were constructed new as
electric tramways. The standard gauge
network was concentrated in the Leiden-Den
Haag-Scheveningen area, whilst the metre
gauge lines radiated out from Amsterdam.
There were two distinct lines in Amsterdam:
that heading north from the north of the Ij
towards Volandam (closed in September
1956) and Purmerend (closed in May 1949),
which had their origins in a 19th century
steam line; and that linking the city with
Haarlem and Zandvoort. This opened, as an
electric route from new, from Haarlem to
Zandvoort in 1899 and from Amsterdam to
Haarlem in 1904. The final closure of the
metre gauge line from Amsterdam was in
August 1957, although an extension of the
urban trams to Sloterdijk two decades later
followed the route of the old NZH line.
Typical of the NZH trams is this bogie car
seen in May 1956. *W. J. Wyse*

NORWAY

Right:

Bergen

The Norwegian port of Bergen possessed a relatively small electric tramway. The first section opened on 3 July 1897 and, by 1917 when the operation was taken over by the local authority, it had expanded to a total of some 10 route km. Following the municipal take-over further investment occurred. However, the system's financial position and the ravages of World War 2 took their toll; one route was closed 'temporarily' in 1943, but was never to reopen. Further closures followed in 1950 and 1957 leaving only route No 1 operational. The western part of that route, to Sandviken, closed in 1961 and the final section, to Minde, in 1965. In July 1958 four-wheel car No 107, dating originally from 1921, is seen heading east towards Minde. *W. J. Wyse*

Left:

Oslo

Whilst a number of routes in the Norwegian capital city have been replaced following the construction of an underground, the tram remains an integral part of public transport provision and the city has seen a number of new trams delivered since 1982. The history of the tram in the city stretches back to a horse tramway that commenced operation on 6 October 1875. Electric tramways first operated on 2 March 1894. The system expanded through to the 1950s and by late 1958 there were 275 power cars and 150 trailers operating over some 80 route km; contraction followed in the 1960s but by the early 1990s there remained seven routes in operation. Höka-built car No 220 (dating from 1953) is seen on route No 1 in May 1961. Apart from the urban network, Oslo can also lay claim to a number of electrified suburban lines. *W. J. Wyse*

Trondheim

The history of the tram in Trondheim is a curious one. The first metre gauge electric tramway opened on 4 December 1901. This was followed by a second route in 1913 and a third in 1927, giving a total of some 13 route km. There was also a separate interurban line, the Gråkallbanen which ran southwest from the town (this opened in 1924 and was taken over by the municipality in 1966 forming part of an extended route No 1). Despite its size the Trondheim system survived through until the 1950s when, in October 1956, the main depot was destroyed by fire. Elsewhere this would have been an opportunity to convert the system, but in Trondheim the fleet was replaced and even a new extension opened. Although two of the three routes were converted to bus operation (in 1968 and 1983) a fleet of 11 articulated trams was acquired in 1984-85 to operate the one remaining route (No 1). However, services were withdrawn on 13 June 1988. Even this was not to be the end of the story as museum trams continued to operate over part of the route until November 1988. August 1990 was to witness a partial reopening of part of the route under the historic Gråkallbanen name. In September 1958 four-axle motor car No 10 (one of a number of trams rebuilt after the 1956 fire) is seen on the loop terminus of route No 3 at Singsaker. *W. J. Wyse*

PORTUGAL

Lisbon

The Portuguese capital possessed an extensive 900mm gauge system which, despite the construction of a metro from the late 1950s (with consequent cut-backs in the extent of the tram system), survives. The first trams in the city were standard gauge mule cars, introduced in November 1873. These were subsequently converted to the 900mm gauge to avoid wear caused by other road users. Electric trams, leased to the British-owned Lisbon Electric Tramways Ltd, first operated on 31 August 1901, and the existing mule-powered system was converted by August 1902. Expansion continued until a final extension in 1958, which took the system to its maximum extent (76 route km). Although threatened in the early 1970s (and taken over by the municipality), the oil crisis of 1974 and a number of particularly narrow streets in the city centre led to the survival of much of the system. However, modernisation, which has been often promised, has yet to take effect, resulting in the continued operation of a remarkable collection of vintage trams. No 343 was the first of a batch of 20 cars supplied in 1906 by the New York firm of John Stephenson; although LET was British-owned, the trams supplied were predominantly imported from the USA. *David Clayre*

Porto (Oporto)

The standard gauge mule trams of Porto, which dated originally from 15 May 1872, represented the first trams in the country. Two years later a second company was established; these were merged in 1893. On 12 September 1895 the company operated its first electric trams. The system remained company-owned until the municipality took over in 1946. A short extension opened thereafter took the system to its maximum size (82 route km and 191 power cars with 25 trailers), but, during the 1950s, it was decided to introduce trolleybuses and the first conversions occurred in 1959. In 1963, it was then decided to convert the entire system over a period of up to 10 years. In the event the closure process has taken a great deal longer and, 30 years on, the electric tram retains a foothold in the town, with just two routes operational in early 1994. On 4 August 1984 one of the system's two-axle cars, No 201 (built in the operator's own workshops c1939), is seen outside the depot. *Andrew J. Fox*

68

SPAIN

Madrid

The Spanish capital city had an extensive tramway network that was, over a number of years, gradually replaced by a metro until final closure came on 2 June 1972. At its peak the system comprised more than 35 routes. Modernisation of the system, including the acquisition of additional PCC-type cars, continued well into the late 1950s. However, by early 1964 the system had contracted to 13 routes with a fleet of 235 trams. By 1967 there remained only seven routes, but the system survived long enough to celebrate the centenary of tramway operation in the city in 1971. Latterly, the only trams to remain in service were the PCC-type cars that were built under licence either in Italy (by Fiat) or in Spain. One of the Spanish-built examples, No 1154, is seen on the last operational route, No 70 from Plaza de Castilla to San Blas, on 11 September 1971. *Paul Collins Collection*

Soller

Situated on the holiday island of Majorca, the short electric tramway linking Soller with Puerto Soller is a remarkable survivor. Built to the strange gauge of 914mm (which was the 'standard' gauge on the island), the 5km-long line opened in 1913. The initial fleet of three power cars was later supplemented with a fourth, with a number of trailers being acquired once the extensive system at Palma (the main town on the island) was abandoned in the 1950s (the final closure of the Palma system came in 1959). Linking Palma and Soller was a 914mm electric railway, which opened in 1912. A typical Soller scene is pictured on 17 October 1971 as car No 2 with a trailer makes its way along the single track route. *Paul Collins Collection*

Right:

Zaragoza

When the final route, No 11, was converted to bus operation in Zaragoza on 22 February 1976 the urban tram became extinct in Spain. Unlike other systems, however, the decline in this city was not the result of an anti-tram policy on the part of the operator but by the refusal of the authorities to renew the operator's lease in the late 1960s unless trams were abandoned. The history of trams in the city stretched back until 1886. The system continued to expand until the 1950s and new or rebuilt cars (including some experimental articulated units) were supplied until the early 1960s. In the late 1950s a total of 13 services operated over 10 routes. The operating franchise was held by the Escoriaza family, who also owned a plant for the construction of trams; the same family was also influential in the importation of second-hand trolleybuses from Britain. On 14 September 1971 bogie car No 307 is seen on route No 11 heading towards Parque San Jose. This was one of a batch of seven built in 1960 using second-hand trucks from La Coruña. *Paul Collins Collection*

SWEDEN

Göteborg (Gothenburg)

Whilst in 1962 Gothenburg was only the second largest tramway in Sweden, with some 297 trams in service as opposed to 405 in Stockholm (out of a total of 880 in the whole of Sweden), trams in the port city of Gothenburg have thrived whilst those in the Swedish capital have all but disappeared. Horse trams first operated in the city in 1879, whilst electric trams first ran in 1902. By 1963, there were some eight routes in operation. As with other Swedish systems, the 1967 change to right-hand running was a major factor, but here the decision was made to retain and develop the tramway. Considerable preplanning went into ensuring the smooth transition; cars were either reconstructed or withdrawn and trackwork modified. Amongst the cars modernised were the 125 of Type M25 (Nos 501-625) which were constructed between 1958 and 1961. Seen at the terminus of route No 5 in May 1961, 'M25' No 528 is seen in its original, non-modified form. Nearly 30 years after the alteration to right-hand running, the tram continues to be a cornerstone of public transport in the city. *W. J. Wyse*

71

Hälsingborg

There have been many reasons for the conversion of a tram system to bus operation, but few were as unusual as that of Hälsingborg in Sweden. The country was the last in mainland Europe to retain left-hand rule of driving and, although public opinion as expressed in a referendum in the mid-1950s recommended retention of the existing rule, external pressure from neighbouring countries in Scandinavia and the growth in international traffic forced the government's hands. Legislation was passed in 1963 with the change to right-hand rule of driving to take place in 1967. It was decided that street tramways in Hälsingborg would be completely converted at the date of change (3 September 1967) and that the system in Stockholm and Malmö would be reduced to a single route. Despite the closure, Hälsingborg's small fleet of cars remained in good condition to the end — as witnessed by this shot of No 29, which dated from 1921 and was subsequently preserved, in August 1967. *Frank Hunt Collection/Courtesy LRTA London Area*

Malmö

Right:

Another system which was, in part, to fall victim to the Swedish change of 1967 was Malmö. Dating originally from the introduction of a horse tramway in the 1880s and with electric trams appearing in the early years of the 20th century, the system in Malmö reached its peak with a network of seven routes. Although four of these had been converted by the late 1940s, three were retained and modernised through the acquisition of new and refurbished cars. The three routes were to survive until the 1960s when, in 1965, the first of the three, No 3, was converted. Route No 1 was converted in September 1967, leaving route No 4, from Sibbarp to Limhamn, in operation. This route was served by the 12 Class G cars dating from the 1940s and a batch of nine trailers built in 1959. However, the single route was not to survive long, being replaced by buses on 27 April 1973. Typical of the Malmö fleet of the early 1950s is four-wheel car No 40 seen in June 1954 on route No 1. *W. J. Wyse*

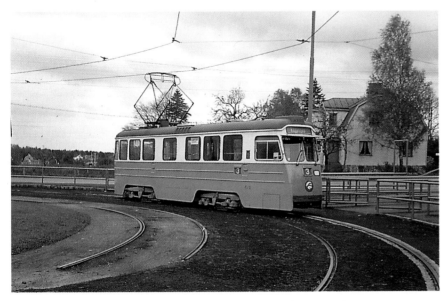

Left:

Norrköping

The small standard gauge tramway in Norrköping dates back to 10 March 1904 when eight two-axle trams were introduced to a single route. The system gradually expanded so that by 1951 it reached its maximum size with a fleet of 63 power cars as well as trailers. The 1950s saw both extensions and the replacement of the bulk of the original route No 1 by new route 3; the remainder became bus operated. In the early 1960s the system comprised three routes, Nos 2, 3 and 4, with 37 power cars. Although one route, No 4, was converted to bus operation on 31 October 1966, the remainder was to survive the change of rule of road in 1967. Norrköping's trams survive into the 1990s and are considered to have a long-term future. In May 1961 Hägglund & Söner-built maximum traction car No 64 was photographed on route No 3. This car was one of 12 delivered in 1958. These cars, although converted for right-hand running, have subsequently been withdrawn. *W. J. Wyse*

SWITZERLAND

Left:
Basel

Situated in the extreme northwest of the country, Basel is a city sufficiently close to both Germany and France to have had international tramway links into both. Although the extra-territorial routes were abandoned during the 1960s, Basel retains the second biggest tramway network in the country with more than a dozen routes and over 200 trams and trailers. The first of the metre gauge electric trams appeared in the city on 6 May 1895 and, at its peak, the system had more than 50 route km. Pictured in August 1984 in Barfusserplatz is Düwag-built No 635 — one of a batch of 56 built between 1967 and 1973 — on route No 7 to Binningen. *Roy Brook*

Right:
Basel (Birseckbahn)

Opened on 6 October 1902 the 6km-long Birseckbahn was originally an independent interurban tramway running south from Basel to Dornach. In 1974 it, and three other lines, were united into Baselland Transport (BLT) with the local bus services in order to integrate public transport in the outer-Basel area. Modernisation of the route — No 10 — was started prior to the establishment of BLT, although the car illustrated here, No 109 (pictured in August 1984), was not actually delivered until 1976. From Dreispitz into the centre of Basel the cars operate over the metals of the municipal undertaking and so, to balance the working, BLT work routes Nos 10 and 11 whilst the BVB operates route No 14. *Roy Brook*

Bern

The Swiss capital of Bern possesses both the remains of an urban tramway system and a number of interurban routes. The metre gauge urban system was inaugurated in October 1890; electric trams first appeared on 1 July 1901 and, at its peak, the system extended over 17 route km. A number of conversions to trolleybus operation reduced the network to three cross-town routes by the early 1980s but tramway extensions, notably to Saali, were also built or planned. The Vereinigte Bern-Worb-Bahnen operates two routes out of Bern to Worb. Initially both these routes operated over the urban network to reach Bern, but the partial conversion of the Bern network to trolleybus means that only one now shares the city tracks; the other now uses a subway. In July 1975 Bern No 114, one of a batch of 15 four-axle cars delivered in 1947-48, is seen heading towards Ostring on route No 5 whilst VBW No 37, one of a batch of three built in 1913 and rebuilt in 1946-58, heads out towards Worb. This section of track still sees dual usage. *Roy Brook*

Geneva

Once the focus of a network of urban and interurban tram routes, the tram network in Geneva had shrunk to a single route — No 12 — during the 1960s as other routes were converted to trolleybus operation. The first trams appeared on the city in 1862 when a standard gauge horse route was established. Metre gauge steam trams also ran in the city (from 1877 until 1911) and the first metre gauge electric cars appeared on 22 September 1894. A privately owned company until 1977, the single route is now under the control of the local authority. In August 1988 No 729, one of a batch of 30 four-axle cars built between 1950 and 1952, is seen heading south towards Bachet — a terminus to which the trams had recently been extended. *Roy Brook*

Trogenerbahn

Linking St Gallen with Trogen, a distance of just under 10km, the Trogenerbahn, with its orange and white trams, is the steepest adhesion tramway in Switzerland. The metre gauge route was first opened on 10 July 1903. During the 1970s five replacement twin-sets were acquired, Nos 21-5, and one of these, No 24, is seen in St Gallen in August 1989. *Roy Brook*

Zurich

The city of Zurich possesses the most extensive tramway network in the country. Standard gauge horse trams were introduced on 5 September 1882 and metre gauge electric trams a decade later on 8 March 1894. Following the municipalisation of the undertaking in 1896 the last horse trams operated in 1900. Although no extensions were opened between 1954 and 1976 the system underwent considerable modernisation during that period with the first articulated car being delivered in 1962. Long term plans envisage the upgrading of some trams routes with subways and the development of an S-Bahn network. The most recent tramcars have been those of the 'Tram 2000' design, such as No 2002 seen here on route No 14 to Triemli — the first route to receive the cars — in July 1981. Authorised in 1974, the first of these low-floor cars was delivered in 1976.
Roy Brook

Back Cover:

Rotterdam

The Dutch seaport of Rotterdam is one of the most important maritime centres in Europe and, as a result, the town is bisected by the River Maas and its associated harbour facilities. The city's standard gauge tramway system suffered significant rationalisation with the construction of a north-south metro and a number of routes, particularly at the south end of the metro, were fortunate to survive. More recently, however, there have been proposals to reintroduce conventional trams to those routes converted earlier and a number of extensions have been built. Horse trams first appeared in the city in 1879, to be followed two years later by steam trams. The first electric trams, operated by the Rotterdamsche Electrische Tramweg Maatschappij, were inaugurated in September 1905. RET was municipalised in 1927. Typical of the Rotterdam fleet is No 363, seen outside the city's Centraal station.
Michael H. Waller

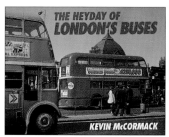
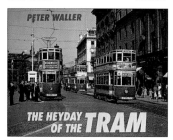

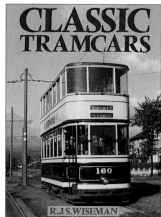
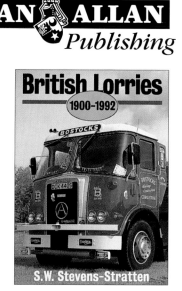